HOW WE LOVE
AND
HOW WE GRIEVE

Poems of You and Me

EDUCO PAARL

DayeLight
PUBLISHERS

ISBN: 978-1-958443-27-9 (paperback)

Illustrations by Roxroy Hutchinson

In Memory Of:

My sister, Sharia Lexan Patterson

My mother, Marlene Rowan Allen

My grandfather, Milfred Allen

and the love that made this book possible.

THE PAARL'S PRAYER

This is a song written in dedication to my sister and mother.

Lord open up my eyes and show me
What I've been doing wrong
I wanna get it right this time, so
Please guide me in Your light.

Take my hand, lead me slowly
Grant me strength and might
Never leave me without grace and mercy
Make my soul shine bright.

I don't know if I will make it to heaven
But I surely have to try
You took my sister and my mother early
Will I be close behind?

So, take my hand, lead me slowly
Grant me strength and might
And never leave me without grace and mercy
You can make my soul shine bright.

So open up my eyes and show me
How to do it right
By guiding me with your light
For maybe then I can make it to heaven.

ACKNOWLEDGMENTS

First and foremost, I would like to show a sincere appreciation to my best friend, Shantal Brown, for her unconditional love, her always open and unbiased opinions regardless of what topic I may put forth, and for always being consistent in my life regardless of the major and minor changes we both experience. Also, for being the first to know about and experience the contents of this book.

A major thank you is due to my cousin, Yanique Carpenter, for giving me a copy of the book "The Art of Seduction by Robert Greene," which encouraged me to shape all the things I say poetically. This, in turn, gave me the best way to calm and express my broken heart.

To a little old lady by the name of Ann Yox, who further encouraged me to "just write, write the poems," I am forever grateful. So, I took her advice and with that of the book to express myself in a poetical manner and so made my way here to a compilation of poems for you and me.

To my dear and close family members who took the time to help me, I am extremely grateful for your love, listening ear, words of encouragement and support. I hope when you read this, you are reminded of how much I am thankful for all you have done and contributed to my life.

The first place I ever publicly expressed poetry was on @on_tha_write_side Instagram page. Therefore, I would like to say a big thanks to the creator, Olia, for creating a place of expression, and for allowing me to share my inner thoughts.

Even though, while difficult, I would like to pay recognition to the person who truly broke my heart and inspired this art; if you ever read this, thank you for being you and loving me in the best way you knew how.

TABLE OF CONTENTS

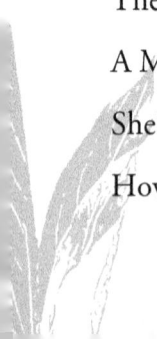

INTRODUCTION

As we grow, we seek to learn about ourselves and try to find ways to express the mixture of who we have come to be at each stage of our lives.

Here, I try my best to express some crucial parts of my late twenties. I still wouldn't say that who I am, even after writing some of these expressions, has changed that much. One thing I can say for sure is that the creativity inside came alive and has now greeted you and me.

Within these pages you may find some of yourself connecting with my soul because we all share experiences with love and grief in our own special way.

Sometimes, I wonder, why do we grieve and in the way that we do? Some would say, however, "How lucky we are to have experienced love than none at all." The pain created from the confusion of not knowing how to love someone who is gone is the grief of love. Let's be honest though, many of us wish to never experience this pain, and whenever we do, we seek to find ways to cope and escape.

Now, here we are, you and me, on the pages of my way to escape the grief of love's frustration.

May you find answers or ways to fill a void or a mind of curiosity, much like me, while going through these pages.

DENIAL OF ATTRACTION

Attraction (noun) is the action or power of evoking interest in or liking for someone or something.

Denial (noun) is the refusal of something requested or desired.

Why try to deny attraction?
Isn't it a necessary satisfaction?
Watch your reactions to its actions.
Tell me after in words of caption,
If it ever led to devastation

"Denying attraction then takes a level of will power and sometimes deep hatred to break."

REJECT ME NOT

I looked at her and found her attractive
I told you of this attraction
Only to hear the shock of your reaction
The embolden words of, "What about me?"

I looked inside my own heart and mind
Of what I knew about you. And,
How could I ever refuse you?
You had always been so kind.

You had changed from the child I knew.
Forward, more sagacious and seductive in your moves
How could I deny the attraction?
I was pulled in and could not refuse.

MY DESIRE

Love is terrifying
But friends we are
So, let's develop the rest.

Building on our trust
Without being in a rush
For it is my desire.

A desire that
We shall last,
To be more than a spark
Though electrifying you are.

WHAT WE HOPE FOR

Little by little you became my center
To the depths of my heart, you entered
Long phone calls and dorm room nights.

And to your friend
that can never erase those sights
I still smile about those hallway lights.

I love to think of black and white
Oh, thee Seacole.
Remember,
that's where we started our roles
Where I hoped you and me could last forever.

We ate cheap meals and exchanged bracelets
As a way to express we cared.

You became my favorite place
The person I had always hoped for
I was happy
Happy with you
For you were my person.

THE SEDUCTION IT BRINGS

Constrict me, five fingers pressed
Motionless are the flood of internal emotions
How can I feel without the pain
Am I a masochist seeking the sadist?

To press and constrict my heart and mind
For the soul to be released
To dismiss the hold upon my body.

The pain and I are a thing
The entwined lovers in a fling
Only I can't hold it as it does me
But, I am still a lover of its hold.

PRESERVING WITHOUT KILLING

Now I have it
How do I keep it?
How to preserve it?
Without killing it?

If I be too nice
If I be too kind
If I be too loving
Will your love die?

If I show emotions
If I even cry
If you see me angry
Will you feel any different?

If I am good
Will you stay with me?
If I am bad
Will you love me more?

Without killing it
Myself and you
How do we preserve it?
A life real and true?

THE PALACE AWAITS

Desirable you are in the prime of your youth
Enthusiastic about the life ahead of you
Jealous you can make them by the lavish you brandish
Harsh though is the known reality,
as it causes the self to enlarge
Anguishing you will be from all you are becoming
Happy you will seek to be from always feeling empty.

Imagining simpler days, you want to be back in
Mourning and tormenting about all that you have scorned
Advantages you had, but deeply took for granted
Navigating through life just to end up at "The Brokens" palace gate
Inviting yourself in while you try hiding all your sins.

Jewels, beautiful and rare, you should know were always held within
Accommodating is the palace with your room awaiting still
Mysterious, such is the thing called life and your experiences of it

Excuse yourself not, even when you can't deduce the truths within.

Satisfaction does come even to those anguishing in sin, so know this is not a hallucination.

HANDS OF TIME

You come and go
Leaving me here
Every day and every night.

You glance at me
Only when you need me
Though I am present with
You always in different forms.

Before the modern days
You needed my hands
as much as the sun
To keep you
From building a rush to run.

I more likely will be here
After you go back to time.

HOLDING ON TO MEMORIES

Can I come with you
  To the places that you go
  So, we may stay close?

If I can't go
Will you miss me?
Taking me in your memories?

If you don't
Just know I will
Become the host.

Holding all the memories
In the place of you
Just so we may stay close.

LIKE A PLANTED SEED

When I plant a seed
I water it
Care for it to grow
As with you and me.

Therefore, I invest in us
Doing my best
Working for things to thrive
To be what we can.

For you know
To survive this land
We all need a hand
So, I give you mine
To bring forth results.

HOW YOU ARE

I t was so subtle
Or maybe I was naïve.

I could not realize
What control
You had over me
What submission to thee.

You are adroit
You can easily convince me
To rejoice
Even in tears of joy
Not meant to be.

DESIRE SPARKED A FIRE

I now like to buy flowers
Which shows me the power of desire.

There is no denial
That love had made its arrival
Because inside me, there was a fire.

I had a desire for your heart
To buy the things you like
To now make special plans
To never extinguish what sparked the fire.

There was a lot to learn
I was willing though
Because you were a main concern
Who had me before I had even known.

A NIGHT IN THAILAND

The time had was crazy
    Let's bound these hands
    Creating different scenes in this land.

Up against the glass you stood
In a way I may see
All of you that commanded me.

Strapped down on the bed
Was the gift of why the flight from Japan
With the legs to be spread.

In this land, a lot was misunderstood
But there were great times
That made us screamed "goddamn."

THE THINGS WE LOVE

You love to sleep in late
I love to watch you sleep
To come over to your side
Just to kiss you on your cheek.

You love to twist your hair
I love the way it looks
The smell when you are near
The glow on your face.

I love to hear you laugh
When you stay up late
And keep me awake
From the shows that you play.

I love the food you cook
I love the juices that you make
I love the taste of everything
All the excitement you create.

NIGHT DRIVES

When the road is clear
    And the night is cool
    I like you by my side
For our night drives.

Sometimes we go shopping
Over to my house
Or even to the beach.

It's the only time
I am never sleepy
As I feel quite alive
Since these nights feel sincere.

THE WRITE OFF

Dismissed by the one you love
Left feeling insignificant
Are the consequences of love
The type of power it evokes.

Yet, how can we deny it
When love is a part of life
Inside the very being we are
Causing parts of us to submit.

A few times there was satisfaction
Maybe even this, you can't deny
Attraction though invited all
The devastation, created from you and me.

BECOMING ANGER

Anger (noun) is a strong feeling of annoyance, displeasure or hostility.

Anger (verb) is to fill (someone) with anger; provoke anger in.

Becoming (adjective) means to be suitable or appropriate.

You thought it wrong
How was it not becoming?
Why was I
to not express such displeasure?

You thought it not provoking
Because,
you kept very silent.

But doesn't hostility come in many forms?
Worst,
when you know not healthy ways for coping?

"Does suppression of your anger make you become a better person, a better judge of another's character though seeming superior through this manner? Tell me, as my actions and anger have deemed me as unbecoming."

THE SECRETS OF DEATH

With death
I told you my secrets
To be the knife to inflict clean cuts
And embolden my self-deception.

To gain affection
Visual perception is your protection
As it's the place you hide
The child that never cried
The one that never freely loved nor trust.

Now here I am
I travel my mind to unravel
The broken pieces of you and I.

INTERROGATIVE QUESTIONS

You want to know my secrets
But, what will you tell me?

You love to search my phone
But, who does it trouble most?

You desire satisfaction
But, how can it be with you pulling away?

You need security and stability
But, why are you afraid of a serious commitment?

You make a deal about values and protection
But, when will things be of real action?

You talk about love and trust
But, where has yours been placed, since not with me?

TRIGGERS

Over a pleasant dinner
An important conversation
Became my trigger
Arising thoughts of how
I knew you did your very best.

It seems; the bigger our desires and fears
The quicker the disappointments
That they bring along with us
Leaving us angry and resentful
Even with the ones we love.

For, in the heat, I did not consider
How we would become bitter
Due to broken hopes and dreams
So now, our blood pulse with heat
Showing a difference from what we once had.

How We Love and How We Grieve

You and I
Are different
Not two peas in a pod.

You show your love through gifts
Lavish gifts when you are feeling rich
Lavish with gifts when you are happy
But, pull away when you are sad
Giving silent treatment
With no show of tenderness.

I show my love through service
Service to my friends and family
Service to you whether happy or sad
I overthink about what to do
I cry and reach out when feeling heavy
Only bearing myself with an overflow of emotions.

With you needing space
Me needing closeness
How could we be?
When we love and grieve so different
Two peas in a pod.

WINE AND WHISKY

I never needed a glass
I drank from the bottles
No chasers needed
To make it easier to drink.

These two poured into me
Allowing me a state of calm
Without a feeling of anxiety.

A father's recommendation
Was best told in "Go have a drink"
To deal with the misery within
So, I drank the wine and whisky
To fight what I felt within.

ANGUISH

On the first day
Without my recognition
Weeks turned into anguish
From a tense situation
With you policing and
Me increasing
An unsubmissive demeanor
To repulse a growing disdain.

Eventually
The universe heard our cries
Of do's and cant's
Which led us to a separation
Whereby you and I will be
Entwined in our remembrance
Of each other.

BLAME AND SHAME

It tears me up that
I tore you apart
In my honest attempt
To find a way to your heart.

One of my deepest shames
That nearly took my name
Was the violation
Which erupted from desperation.

Now I am
Without the am
Because I blame
Who I am.

PENANCE

My thoughts grew unholy
As I knew
Not why I was punished slowly.

To redeem myself
And cause no harm
I turned towards penance
As it was the only way
To tame my own vengeance.

For, you do not know
True protection, because
It's not of your reflection.

For a mirror of you I am not
But to you I brought a lot
Though unseen to your eyes.

FIGHT WITH ME

Hold me close when you get angry
Don't shut me out and contain yourself
within
Yell at me and let me know you are still with me
Let me see your tears so
I may dry them.

Fight with me and do not stay silent
Just do something
To let me know you are still with me
Don't just buy me gifts
To fix me how you want me.

Express to me words without condescending
Fight with me in a way
That shows me you care and still love me
Do not step out like you always do
Just because I am tending.

Being an avoidant makes you flee, but
Fight with me and never leave
So, let me know you are still with me
As I anxiously sit and wait for you to reach me
While mending my broken pieces.

NO OBLIGATION

Together we are but far we are
With little decency
Living in a house of scars.

Our parents and their shaping
We are forever lovers raging.

So, to the naïve
You owe no obligation
To share no whereabouts of your location
While taking fancy trips towards the ocean
To return and create an instant commotion.

Neither you nor I
Could ever believe
What a thought
Of having no obligation
Could really set in motion.

We are both just lucky though
I like to seek other suggestions
To help clear deep temptations
And to make all fair and square
So, we both may experience peace and growth.

PEARLS AROUND YOUR NECK

Not a fight did you make
There was no resistance
Only a sense of relief to be yourself.

You sat with the Brazilian short cut on your head
Pearls around your neck
With me saying to myself how amazing you looked.

You prepared for that interview
Spoke boldly of all that you would do
Without even thinking of me.

You desired to be with those strange men
Maybe so they could buy you real pearls
I don't really know.

You looked gorgeous, though
My rage just could never say those words
As I realized you cared only about yourself.

CAN I BREAK IT MYSELF?

Sometimes I am so angry
But for what my mind would do
Society would want to hang me.

There are times though
I want to break it myself
To see you be the one in pain.

For you to know real hurt
No matter how it came
For now, to me, you were the worst.

A cold distant unappreciative girl
Holding on to anger through pride
Never remembering any good.

OFFENSIVE FIGHT

When I was young
A family friend often
Repeated this one phrase
"Walk away from trouble when you can."

This one time I dared not
As I grew tired of your ways.

I tried pleading and
To bite my own tongue
This was not enough.

I sprung into a rage
With heavy words
Roaring from my lungs
Then, early principles became undone.

WAS THERE ANY LOVE?

Was being me ever enough?
Was there really any love?

I look back and all I see
Is the rough path between you and me.

To you, I was experimental
So, with everything you were judgmental
Only being essential for sex and to fill an empty space.

What could ever help us?
When you are easily embarrassed or jealous.

This break-up threw me
Not because I felt used
But because I was angry with myself not you.

AM I THE TOXIC ONE

To express myself
I sometimes yell
I might swear at you
From becoming angry.

It seems unfair
To label this toxic
As we all show our cares
And pain in different ways.

I might be toxic though
As many times
We are not our normal selves
Which leaves us to think
About who we really are.

BARGAINING WITH DISILLUSION

Bargaining (verb) is when we discuss/negotiate terms and conditions of something in order to get to an agreement that is of a suitable advantage to ourselves.

Disillusion (noun/verb) is the disappointment experienced from the resulting discovery that something is not as good a one believed it to be.

Reality can be hard-hitting
Leading to severe stages of bargaining
While trying to clear the confusions
Created from the devastations of attraction.

"I know not if you bargained for me, but for you, I did with God and the universe, time and time again."

25 KISSES

Coming off the fire strong
 Was me each time
 As you often thought
You had been wronged.

So, for this, I learned for you
How to make a sincere apology.

After failing quite a few times
Due to your psychology
I gave 25 kisses on the last try
As I was sorry I ever made you cry.

Yet, in the end, I found out the hard way
It was never forgiven
Only left inside you, to sit
Until the next fire was lit.

RESCIND

The wind blew in the house
All windows closed, it was cold
It was the chide bestowed
Which made it so.

Only pondered, I pondered
While you wondered
Leaving no thought nor place of me.

Please rescind that which is not of love
So warmth can radiate
For in the house
It now greatly hurt.

UNDESERVING DEATH

I hurt because
I had to watch us die
With you being heartless
My heart ached
Followed by my mind.

With prolonged silence
I yearned for your adoration
Leading myself to
The depths of desperation.

Help and intervention I sought
My own knowledge proved weak
As salvation was needed
As I laid in the shadow of death
Overcame by my own anxiety.

My suffering made me ask
When will it end?
For this love could not contend
This was an undeserving death.

DID I DISPLEASE YOU

Dig deep down
Determine another destiny
Don't put us to death.

Dear sweet darling
Do see my dedication
Do we deserve death?

Did my best displease you?
Did the dew not fill the dam?
Dazed, was I really?

Did the gifts at your door
Die before their expiration date?
Doomed for the dumpster.

Destined, much like the love I have
Daring my heart to keep it
Despite the deep distress.

Dreaming now, in a gold Nissan
Destinations of spectacular satisfaction
Demolishing slowly every devastating displeasure
created.

IN WAYS WE MAY

May I come to know thyself
In ways one had wished to know thee
May our memories not haunt me
Due to the nonchalant past.

May your present be true to you
In ways that I could not
And heal your heart
With a single shot.

May the future be your oyster
In ways high for you to gallop
And me... May I be
The pearl lost at sea.

THE HEAVENS

I think the heavens hear me
It sends the rain to calm me
Dripping and splashing at my window sills
It's the light noise to my night's loneliness.

As my mind cries out
To the heavens for wings
To be an angel to visit
And leave earth
To caress those whom are beloved.

Oh, why do I despair?
When the mind is fortified with gratitude
The heart with love
And the soul, of an appreciated
Home in heaven.

My body ceases to be unified
As my mind reaches towards heaven
My soul prepares the way
As my heart makes its break.

TINKERED DREAMS

I tinkered with the dust
Hoping it would make me fly.

The rust from these
Old pipes though
Will only affect my lungs.

But, I never guessed
This was the only way
I would ever leave this land.

Covered under a bread pan
To grow no more
Just to become the dust
From which it all began.

OPPOSITES OF A MAGNET

How do I talk about it
When you want to talk about it?
How do I release these emotions of words
not easily spoken?
How can I shed these tears in a way to let you hear me
and see me clearly?
How can I be strong while seeming weak and seeking?

How do you not cry or see a way to dry my eyes?
How can you be okay with leaving, and condemn me
for believing?
How can you just criticize while I empathize?
How do you see yourself; do you bend on your knee to
know?

How is this our journey with you having power of
attorney?
How will we resolve all that has dissolved?
How do we feel whole with only half our souls?
How can we be communicative without being
defensive?

How can we be, do and feel once more?

CHANGING ROLES

What if our lives were different?
Would it be a life that is magnificent?

What if you wore my shoes?
Would all this tension between us diffuse?

What if you bore my pain and remorse?
Would you have gained the strength to change our
course?

What if you loved me like I loved you?
Would you now easily forgive all that has been done?

What if you lost all you cared for within a few years?
Would you still not bare yourself and show your tears?

What if parts of you were never broken?
Would your short-housed love for me have been
awoken?

What if we were never just two girls?
Would there ever be you and me in written words?

What if we just could answer these "Woulds?"

Would we change roles without detours?

FEVERISH DREAMS

Where is he?
Why are you with me?
Is it the fever?
That creates these dreams?

Or
Is it this need within us?
A need to feed on you
As you feed on my self-esteem?

It's hard
Hard for me to believe!

Take me out of this dream
Take this vicious pain from my head
Let my eyes open
And my grief be over.

Set me free
Set me free from my feverish dreams.

LET'S GO BACK

That night it rained
While we took the train
Towards the mountains
To the hot springs of Hakone.

On the train I cried
Due to how I felt inside.

Why was I again deprived?
Of all the hopes inside.

Let's go back
Before the train ride.

When all felt fine
With you by my side
Without all the phone calls
I now hate to recall.

DELUSIONAL THOUGHTS

Crossing the streets
Was it you hiding from me?
Was it just my thoughts?
I paused, wondering and laughed
Were these delusional thoughts?

Was this a moment
Where we were feeling dreaded?
A past created
Disdain to walk the same path
Truly is this you and me?

Answers, they may come
But, for now, I can't believe
This is who we are
Avoidant strangers hiding
So, there is no reuniting.

LIFE IS CONFUSING

Deep inside there is a desire
Much more like a yearning
It's not fully understood
However, it brings the melancholy.

It makes me feel sad
Leaving me to want a place
Just to be alone.

These thoughts are heavily occurring
So, I hope I learn about myself
While with time, to show
Much discernment and contentment.

LOVE ME ONCE AGAIN

I admired you
From the first time we met.

You ended up
Following me home
It wasn't hard to imagine
What for
As you had
Made your intentions known.

You were kind
The sweetest I had ever known
Genuine care and such consideration
I had never yet known.

When you held me
And took me off the floor
It was warm
A feeling much unknown.

When you held me
It was like I was loved
A warm embrace
I was so afraid to conform.

Now here I am
Hoping
You will love me once again
Knowing it's unrealistic
Since I mourned you years ago.

OPEN CONSIDERATION

I am poor with my words
But, come let us work it out
This love is only beginning
There is much room for growth.

How may I show you
All that you are to me?
Without you present
To do all that I can.

Come with an open mind
Come with an open heart
Come knowing you are loved
Let me know this is an illusion.

Rovoy Hutchinson
2023

LASTING DEPRESSION

Depression (noun) is a feeling of severe despondency and dejection.

Lasting (adjective) is enduring or being able to endure over a long period of time.

Where did the time go?
Did I sleep through it
As a way to fight feeling low?

Will the melancholy stop?
I must admit
I don't know.

Such conflict
Makes it hard
To ever stop feeling low.

"With this realization I feel more alone; yearning for death to come and take all that's left of me, as a way to rid the void of what is deeply missing in me."

ALONE

Slowly, something came
To replace the space of you.

Disillusion resulted from being alone
No bargaining could help
I am now melancholy's own.

I could no longer fight
I had inflicted wounds.

Love was not preserved
So, inside to myself I turned
Going over memories
Considering different ends.

THE REALIZATION

You might feel it
For I know I surely do
Cause, look at me
I suffer these wounds
As the clutter of thoughts intrude.

You always come back
This time is different though
I'm realizing
As you cut me no slack
I feel more alone
Fighting on my own.

Utilizing past mistakes
We both try to use
In different ways
To create our own escapes.

LEAVE ME BY THE DOOR

I want to smoke my cigarette
As all I want is to forget.

So, when I pass out
Don't wake me
Just leave me by the door.

As it's not your attention I seek
Nor your further critique.

I am at a point filled with regret
While looking for a way to be still
As I know my life is in dismay and can't reset.

MY CARES

Within a year my cares died
The womb from which I came
A love I held so dear
The inches that reached my waist
And myself I thought I knew.

Within a year, places changed
From a space in your heart
To countries and miles apart
Being disgraced without your embrace.

Within a year all moods the same
Me filled with shame
As I lay claim to the blame
Which inflamed my cares to die
Leaving none to spare.

YOU AND ME

Where did the responsibilities come from?
They really caught me off guard
We were living together now
Finally, a dream came through
However, it went quicker than it came.

I became overwhelmed, almost dumb
I was now caught in a discard
Was this the crop from seeds sowed?
Is this what I had spent years to pursue?
To become quickly a person inflamed in shame?

You outgrew me quicker than I knew
Leaving behind feelings of a lasting disregard.

LOVE DEEPLY MISSING

I never got to meet you
You made me happy though
I beamed with excitement
From the thought of you.

Already, I miss you
I was looking forward to meeting you
To smile at you as you smile at me.

To fill you with the love
I am deeply missing
You will never know me
But I will remember you.

TWO LIVES IN ONE

From two I came to be
Knowing life has no guarantee
Simply living and trying
I wanted two lives from one.

In the one they found not
Two heartbeats of little ones
In just weeks it's a lot
Life has taken my true love.

THE FRIENDS WE LOVE

Am I your partner or even a friend?
Are the friends you love real?
As I never saw them where you needed them.

You said you could have done it all on your own
Did you belittle their efforts to you as you did mine?
Was me being there for you worth nothing?

Did the trips and the brunches make them enough?
Were they beside you when you were on crutches?
Such is life, but only one was there with me.

To me, you supported them more than you did me
You gave them your energy and your space
Never wanting me around and always counting my
mistakes.

DAMAGES OF A BEING

It's an empty hole
Not the ones you see
But of what I see
From the looks of a mirror
Or reflection.

You see an existence
But I see what's not seen
The gaping loneliness
And the emptiness of someone
You think whole.

The parts that should be
To form its mold
The maker and its maker
Kept something from
Its structure.

And like fine wine
It aged in structure
To become a vulture
To fill the hole from
Anyone who hugged her.

A BROKEN CHILD

Am I a broken child?
Are scars from the past still with me?
Is it what cries out to you for love?
How does it survive inside?

My therapist, she tried
To remind me of what I was deprived
She prescribed ways to heal this broken child
To Better Help the pain building inside.

She advised as I analyzed
All this pain that was in disguise
Masking what resided deep inside
Yearning for a love which it could no longer hide.

HOME FEELS UNKNOWN

I am home, to a place I know
But without you it feels unknown.

You are not here to greet me
To make things feel like a party
To be the bigger of the two.

It took me some time
I know you missed us both
But I came home and sat beside you
Though I went to see her first
As it was just hard to see you this way.

In this way I realized
I lost you to lose her to lose you
So, in all we arrived to this unknown.

ACME OF EUPHORIA

How can I escape?
Through the tiny whites
And euphoria foe?

These sensual desires
Of momentary acme
Which captures deeply
The split-ness of the soul.

Lingering over you
Are the heavy breaths
Of a debtful soul
Looking to collect
From a man like you.

Clothed, but naked
In a cloud of white
I entered a state
Of pure delight.

Escaping the foe
Through the euphoria bestowed

In a bliss of no awareness
It has me to itself.

FOREHEAD

By the old Fort
Painted is
A magnificent butterfly.

Leave me standing
Strap my arms to it
Aim for my forehead
With a single shot
Shoot me dead.

Bringing a warm red
What an artistic end
Where the lover lies
Strange doors led
To my other life.

This is how it opened
Through thoughts described
Isn't it just colorful
The way ahead
Just like I have said.

Can't you see it?
I have changed

Watch me flutter, like
Other spirits in disguise.

IN THREE DIMENSIONS

In the house, I spoke to myself in three dimensions
There was the me at the door
Watching the most impactful moments of my past
While envisioning my future to come.

I saw us at the dinner table and lying in bed
All while standing at the doorway between the two
Oh, how I wished I could
Change the me you looked at then
The sad and angry me.

The night at the dinner table, I walked out
A few hours later, I stood at the same doorway
Looking at you sound asleep
In that moment, I thought of how much
I wished you had cared enough
That you could not sleep.

Instead, I took to the next room
Overwhelmed by sadness and grief
Suppressed into deep music
Further awakened my own despair
To escape, I took to my hair a scissors from our home.

Hours later my head
Was clearer than the day I entered this world
What took me over ten years
Was gone through despair
What you saw the next day when you awoke
Was the baby alien you could never forgive.

You grew more and more to hate me
As I waited for you.

You left me without a goodbye and
Took my mind right along
This created the three dimensions
And I saw my ways to kill you.

My love was however not evil
And turned inwards to save you
So, one night in the next room
Overwhelmed by sadness
I took a belt and pulled it tightly
Until I laid there still
Seeing them both with me
And crying out to meet them.

Now, I see them often
The me, death and love.

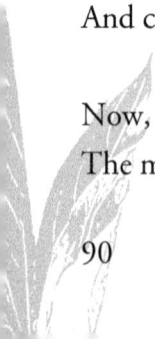

HARD FOR ME TO TELL

What is love?
This is hard for me to tell
When there has been tension everywhere I dwell.

Could it be me?
This is hard for me to tell
As sometimes I leave places leaving in a yell.

Might it be you?
This is hard for me to tell
As you never yelled in the place we dwelled.

Do I know love?
This is hard for me to tell
Sometimes I think I do, then start to feel unwell.

Will we have love?
In a way that it may excel?
This is hard for me to tell.

Might the universe have new intel?
It seeks to expel
Maybe then this is not hard for me to tell.

SMILING FROM A DREAM

You are gone
It's so hard
You were right here
When did you move beyond?

Beyond the life of presence
Where we could meet
Where we could speak
Where we could share an embrace.

How could time turn you cold
Your existence only to be short-lived
Now, I only see you in my dreams
Simply smiling back at me.

You look happy
Even though it's just a dream.

Did you see her?
I hope you did
I hope you both found peace.

THEY ALL MADE ME

Who would I be?
Be without them
Without them to shape me.

Who would I be?
Without my mother's hard work
Without her constant departures.

Who would I be?
Without my father and his sins
Without being unable to trust him.

Who would I be?
Without these eyes to see my sister
To see her and all her troubles.

Who would I be?
Without you all
Without all your different ways
And experiences to shape me.

Who would I be?
Without you, breaking my heart
Without the pain, to face who I am

How I was made to be.
Who would I be?
If I didn't ask this now
How am I sure they all made me?

Who am I?
What will I be?
Am I me or different parts of you?

PAIN TOUCHES MY DREAMS

Where do I survive?
Is the place outside my head?
Sometimes I am not sure I'm alive.

I know in the end
I like it when I'm asleep
It stops the knives from reaching these veins.

Pain touches my dreams
As my brain still thinks of you
Leaving me to think, where to survive.

THE PLACE WE ARE

To help ease
The bouts of sharp pain
I like to go
To the river
Near the apartment
To watch the carps.

Hearing the flow
Of the streams
Does something to me
I guess it calms me.

Sometimes being there
Makes me wonder
What would it be like?
If I was something different
Not human, but like water
Or the wind.

How different and easy
It will be to move and change
From the place we are.

THE THREE OF YOU

I hate how I miss you so
How the sudden sadness comes on at times.

Each time I know which of you
Brings the most sadness
Yet, no matter what
I can't help but cry.

Especially on nights or days like these
When I just feel sad.

It never lasts though
And these days I just write of you
Whichever one of you comes to me.

DEATH IS SELFISH

Please stay beside me
Don't be selfish sleeping long
Wake and be with me.

Everything changes
Death seems to take everyone
Nothing stays the same.

I look at pictures
They show me all the stages
Now left far behind.

ALL THAT IS LEFT BEHIND

All the scars reside in me
Left by youth and you.

People observe them slowly
In my behavior
Learning of them they don't help.

They create more scars
Leading me further inside my mind.

ACCEPTANCE OF COMMITMENT

Acceptance (noun) is the process of receiving something as adequate, valid or suitable.

Commitment (noun) is a state or quality of being dedicated to a cause, activity, etc. that can restrict freedom of action.

Note:

"We are all obligated to something, and the sooner we accept that, the easier the path."

Through devastation we see a flawed reality
Seeking out the pleasures of the past for normality
Only to realize self-commitment leads to true fulfillment
The sooner the acceptance the lesser the external expectance.

"Accepting that love and grief are like conjoined twins, we can make a commitment to a process of seeking out an adequate fulfillment as we experience the different stages of our reality."

HOW I FOUND IT

I grieved, I grieved, I grieved
Till I grew weary and sought out contentment.

Here I found different versions of myself
The emotional, the cold, and the contented.

I spent time with myself
Fasting and praying to deal with my grief.

Things still do come and go
But I am a lot better now
Slowly accepting this new self and reality.

OH JAMES – THE SONG OF A BROKEN HEART

Oh, James
Why did you leave?
Why did you left
Her with a broken heart?
Could you not stay?
Was the love not true?
Did she not fill your cup
As much as you wanted from her?

What did you need?
Why did this love break
So many times for her?
But not for you?

Was the love not true?
Why did you
Came and went
So many times
Just as you pleased
Without thinking of her?

Now she has no room
This time for you

She wants your name
Out her heart.
Oh, James
She loved you so damn hard.

Now this is goodbye
And the door is closed
She has filled your cup
For the final time.

Now leave her alone
And let her be
So her heart can mend
And find new love, this time.

THE LOVE BIRD'S STORY

I laid on the floor passed out
The effects of everything
Had worn me thin.

However, your presence
I sensed and the sound of a shutter
You called my name and told me of the mess I made.

I got up and continued to the floor of my room
To which I continued the momentary escape
Of my present existence.

You cleaned my mess
While in your head
You saw me as just a pest
To where you could no longer nest.

You felt unsafe and thought
To me, you could not attend
So, you moved your heart
From our home and into his own.

Now, here again, upon the floor

I lay writing of a time no more
In the house I thought our home.

A MUSE GAVE ME PLENTY

I barely talk about you
  I rarely say your name.

Now you are a muse
An idea for my book.

Back then, I had no money
Maybe that's why you left.

Now you are the reason
Why I have plenty you see.

Don't try to sue me for this book
As no part was ever funny.

Just be happy you got an advance
And in the end, you made me wealthy.

Seriously though, don't lawyer up
Oops, I forgot! You are now the lawyer.

SHE'S WITHOUT

Across from you I sat
I became crossed-eyed
To make a funny face for
You to smile.

As I cycled in my head across
Countries and seas
To be where
I truly wished to be
Right back to a time where
You greeted me.

At the door as I rushed to
Cover my distress
You've always been with
Me, and now these
Two almost three years have
Been too long.

Without your smell
And your presence
To numb my current existence.

HOW SHE BECAME

I met a girl
She could dance
She seemed so fun and alive.

But deep inside
Her love dare not dance
For memories from a past
Had stepped too hard
On her young heart.

They stepped as she stepped
Harder and harder
Increasing the power of
A loveless heart.

Triggering my own hurt
And worst a yearn
For the urge
From which I came.

To write of our encounters
Was the only way
I could think to expel
My own inner demons

Created from a broken heart.

CONVERTING WITH TIME

I am moving on, just not sure how fast
From time to time, you are on my mind
I know to you, we were never meant to last
It amazes me though, how quickly I am behind.

Sometimes I think of when I wanted to die
The actions and reasons which created the why
I am here right now mystified as to the cause I am alive
I do give credit to God and my family no matter how
unjustified.

I am a currency, one high in value, though you knew
not the worth
This is my first proof, one you might surely try to
dispute
Seeing how much it began and came back to you
All these words are attached to you, and you are its true
birth I must affirm.

CREATION OF A NEW

I have an ego, which is the alter of
All the shame I carry
Where I am free to mold myself anew
To the me I truly wish to be.

The one who is whole
Without the need for validation
The one who feels not abandoned
As the self is complete.

The ego formed from
The lack felt every time
You came and went.

Since now, you are no more; it seeks out
The source of the initial need for approval.
To which it can cut
The hold from the child that it has came.

So, it may now be its own independent soul
Without the known of broken hearts
Or the grooming from other
Broken parts from which the child was molded.

A REALITY CREATED BY THOUGHTS

What are my thoughts?
If not to learn from
To look at the past
For ways to understand.

What is reasoning?
Without deepening my senses
So as to cause less offenses
And to make us be one.

What matters my truth?
Without thoughts of reality
Created by our youth
To form a sense of actual practicality.

I see the sense
Of your reality
By pausing to reason.

IT TOOK ME SOME TIME TO SAY

It took me some time
I was wrong
With more days to come
I will still be wrong.

I caused a mess
That now prolongs
Which makes me
Sing somber songs.

It took some time
For the right way to come along
To express
How sorry I am.

Know you are strong
That I am sorry
To have caused the fight
Please know I was wrong
Even though
We will never reunite.

MOVING ON

It's funny how
I am moving on
Yet still, I think of you.

I try to analyze the thoughts
Without judging or criticizing
Why you cross my mind.

Sometimes I stop
In moments we shared
Just looking around.

Sometimes I am on the street
Sometimes in a room, just you and me
Or just having KFC by the beach.

Then the moments fade
Bringing me back in the instant
To continue my journey moving on.

IT HAD TO BE

I loved the start
And I still do to this very day
Even if I am laying cold in my grave
As you read through in ease.

The end though
It makes me sad, no matter how much I understand
It had needed to be
Because, after all, without it
How could I ever write about You and me
For you to read?

Without the parts in between
The start and the end
We would have no story, no existence
So, for that, I would never regret
Our start, the rocky journey in between
and most definitely not the end.

Instead, I have come to appreciate
You even more
The way you were
The way you are
And me

With all the me I was never am for you.
How our story together was perfectly imperfect
Because it created a whole book of poems
Of you and me.

ABOUT THE POET

Tammy, a friend of mine, once said to me that I could be described as her happy sad friend. This perspective is truly dependent on you not me, but I would say that the Earth was truly blessed on a day in April 1993 when I came to be.

I hope from these poems and the one written below that you may come to know about me and be free to shape a perspective of your own and maybe write it back to me.

REMNANTS OF ME

Naked are my bones
As I am without flesh.

Alive without a heart
I still move about with ease.

For these bones are a show
Of my strength from all I endured.

I am a thankful poet and to you I would like to express my gratitude for reading each word and for connecting with me.

www.ingramcontent.com/pod-product-compliance
Lightning Source LLC
Chambersburg PA
CBHW071139090426
42736CB00012B/2169